MW01169407

WEALTH
BEYOND
DEBT

MONEY MAX PRO
DEBT TO WEALTH SYSTEM

THE ULTIMATE GUIDE TO BUILDING
FINANCIAL SECURITY

JASON INGRAM, IAR

FOREWORD BY
JOHN WASHENKO & SKYLER WITMAN

Copyright © 2024 United Financial Wealth.

All rights reserved. No part of this publication may be reproduced, distributed or transmitted in any form or by any means, including photocopying, recording, or other electronic or mechanical methods, without the prior written permission of the publisher, except in the case of brief quotations embodied in critical reviews and certain other noncommercial uses permitted by copyright law.

United Financial Wealth/Wealth Beyond Debt
Printed in the United States of America
moneymaxaccountpro.com

United Financial Wealth
120 E 13065 S Draper, UT 84020
Draper, Utah

Although every precaution has been taken to verify the accuracy of the information contained herein, the author and publisher assume no responsibility for any errors or omissions. No liability is assumed for damages that may result from the use of information contained within.

Wealth Beyond Debt/ Jason Ingram -- 1st ed.

ISBN 9798320829340 Print Edition

CONTENTS

AUTHOR'S NOTE

As I'm finishing the writing of this book, I'm often awake in the early morning wondering, "What did I forget?" There's always something I think I might have done differently or explained another way to be more precise and clear.

I've written two successful books on wealth – *Accelerated Wealth* and *Accelerate Your Impact*. I've met with hundreds of families and assisted them in strategies to build wealth. People like a plan. Engineers, airline pilots, physicians, teachers—you name the profession—all have plans and try their best to follow and execute those plans.

Prevailing thoughts on debt and wealth have been the same for many years. All the talking heads tell us we must first get rid of our debt and our superfluous spending; we must gain control of our budget. Some even suggest we rent out a room in our home. Only then can we begin to go about building wealth for retirement.

I'm afraid I have to disagree—and until the Money Max Pro Debt-to-Wealth System, I would have agreed with those people. Would it be crazy to think that you could build wealth and simultaneously eliminate debt by using the same dollar for both?

This incredible software turns the tables and converts hope into a genuine and powerful strategy. You can eliminate your debt and build wealth simultaneously, using the same dollar twice!

Sit back and get ready to have some of your beliefs and ideas turned upside down. Suppose you get engaged and follow the system. In that case, you will not only eliminate your mortgage, student loans, and all your debt faster than you could even have imagined but also create a private pension fund for yourself when you retire that has tremendous tax advantages.

My son, Ayric, began his first career as a cook by making biscuits at the YMCA camp near our home in Florida. The chef, Jerry, helped to give him a passion for seeing the joy in people's faces when they ate one of his creations. Ayric toiled as a cook and eventually became a sous chef and executive chef at several of the best restaurants in Hawaii, Alaska, Michigan, Wyoming, and finally, a Colorado resort. But he grew tired of the late nights and difficulties of running a restaurant. He decided to return to the university and study his real passion, computers. He (with the assistance of student loans) completed a Bachelor of Science degree in IT Security and now has an exciting position with a firm where he excels and continues to grow.

We supported him emotionally and spiritually, but he wanted to do it himself financially. He graduated two years later at the age of thirty-eight, owing around $50,000 in student loans. Under the bank's plan, he would have been finally out from under the yoke of his student loans at age forty-eight. Ayric plugged into the Money Max Pro Debt-to-Wealth System and is now one year out of college. After purchasing an almost new Subaru for $27,000 and paying off the student loans, he will be completely debt free in 2.3 years and have a tax-advantaged retirement fund, producing about $56,000 a year for 35 years if he chooses to retire at age 55.

He's just one example of the power of the Money Max Pro Debt-to-Wealth System. There are countless families around the country who are on track to not only eliminate their debt in one-third to one-half the tine, but to build a powerful tax-advantaged retirement.

Too good to be true? Read and see for yourself. Carpe Diem!

Jason Ingram

FOREWORD

When Skyler Witman and I started our business in 1998, we wanted to help families. We started our mortgage company, funding it with our savings and credit cards. We believed that if we built a reputation for having the best rates and service, word would spread, and good things would come from that. Gratefully, this proved to be correct. As our company grew, we began to see an alarming pattern. People continued to create debt over and over again. We had too many return clients. It was distressing, and we knew there had to be a solution. In 2006, **United Financial Freedom (UFF)** and the **Money Max Account** were born. It is a solid way to assist families in eliminating debt and to stop digging such deep holes. We rolled it out to a small test group and were astounded by the results. It worked! Since its inception, the **Money Max Account system has paid off $2.5 billion in consumer debt with $9 billion in debt under management.**

Fast forward to 2024. After additional research and extensive further development of the Money Max Account system, we are pleased to announce an exciting upgrade: **the Money Max Pro Debt-to-Wealth System**. This system can eliminate a family's debt in one-third to half the time and simultaneously build wealth for retirement. It's truly revolutionary.

The booklet you are about to read is brief, yet it outlines what we believe to be the most powerful financial tool for the families we have ever seen. It's just math, and it works.

Retirement has become complex and requires careful planning. In 1960, the average man lived to the age of 66.6 years. Today, an average American man has a life expectancy of 78.93 years—more than a decade longer! For someone born today in 2024, the average life expectancy is projected to be 88.78 years, meaning another decade of life and, therefore, another decade of retirement to fund. Retirees are searching for retirement income that is dependable and secure. They need to better manage taxes before and during retirement.

Most importantly, they seek to protect their principal, representing a lifetime of work and gratification. For some, it has been well planned. For others, it is financial fear and dread. Regardless of circumstance, retirement is in a category unto itself. A thousand small decisions regarding saving and deferring gratification are the cornerstone. Working, saving, spending, and career moves are all critical. Without lifestyle behavioral decisions during our earning years, there will be few assets upon which to retire.

Overwhelmingly, Americans also seek help—professional, experienced, thoughtful advice. The investment advice is not necessarily confusing, but to the retired engineer, small business owner, teacher—or any of us—it may be so. Therefore, help can be the difference between a comfortable and stressful retirement.

The Money Max Pro Debt-to-Wealth System is designed to guide you to debt-free living and create a path to a comfortable retirement. Skyler and I envision that many families we continue to help will have no debt, and now, with this upgrade, the Money Max Pro Debt-to-Wealth System can help them build wealth and a stress-free retirement.

Jason Ingram joined UFW as our Chief Strategy Officer in 2021 after he sold his financial services practice in St. Louis and had a very short retirement. His expertise in life insurance and other financial tactics and strategies was just what we needed to take UFW to the next level.

I hope you enjoy this book as much as I have. Remember, *applied* knowledge is power! Take heed. Make a plan. Follow the plan. Enjoy your retirement.

John Washenko & Skyler Witman
Co-Founder UFF & UFW

INTRO

*When would you want to know if what you thought was true
turned out not to be?*

IT'S 2 A.M. The house is quiet. The kids are sleeping peacefully in their bedrooms. Your wife is softly snoring next to you. You're exhausted, but your mind won't quit racing. You toss and turn. You quietly get up and check your bank statement on the computer again. For most of us, it's money that keeps us up at night worrying. When couples have a fight or heated discussions, it's almost always about money: worrying if your 401(k) will drop again like last year; worrying about how you will be able to pay for the kids' college; worrying about your job and inflation. Even though you are only forty, you wonder if you'll have to work forever because you don't have enough saved for retirement or a plan to save more. You may worry about debt. You don't have a tremendous amount of credit card debt—only a few thousand dollars—but the two cars, the student loans you're *still* paying on after fifteen years, and the mortgage. You bought the house a few years back when mortgage rates were about 3 percent. Money was cheap, so you might have purchased a home just a bit more expensive than you really could afford. But, man, it had a great backyard, was in a perfect area, and the wife and kids loved it.

All you want is for the wheel to stop turning as you lie awake. You know you need a guide, someone to act as a sounding board, some way to navigate through the complicated world of finances and help you to see that you are on track. Some ways to make changes when your world changes, like when you get a pay raise, have an extra expense, or contemplate going on a family vacation. Can you afford it?

Now, exhausted, you fall asleep, but when you awaken, the endless chatter picks up without a hitch: what if, what if, what if?

THE LION AND THE GAZELLE
WHICH ARE YOU

"Every morning in Africa, a gazelle awakens. It knows it must run faster than the fastest lion, or it will be eaten.
Every morning, a lion wakes up. It knows it must outrun the slowest gazelle, or it will starve to death.
It doesn't matter whether you are a lion or a gazelle . . . when the sun comes up, you'd better be running!"

A LION KNOWS what it must do daily to feed itself and survive. It has clarity of goals (eating or starving), a plan (stalk gazelles), urgency (I'm hungry now and will be hungrier later), and purpose (to capture its prey). And the lion monitors its progress—is the belly full today?

A gazelle knows it must run to save its life and for survival; it is always on the defense. All it knows is that the lion is after him and that it must run. The gazelle must outrun or outsmart the lion to survive. What if it does just get up to run but happens to run the wrong way? No second chances. A lion can go a day without eating, but the gazelle gets no second chance. The gazelle is running with no sense of purpose or plan—it is running to survive.

The analogy of the lion and the gazelle is not unlike the present-day world of retirement planning. We are either lions or gazelles and often just run without an idea of the course. We don't want to be eaten, or we are so hungry we can hardly stand it.

The modern system of financial planning utilized by 98 percent of financial advisors needs to be fixed. We are all anxiously waiting for a possible next 2001–2002 or 2007–2009. "How much will I lose?"

We look like gazelles in the headlights. It doesn't have to be this way.

According to the EBRI Retirement Security Projection Model developed in 2003 and updated numerous times, an estimated 40.6 percent of all U.S. households headed by someone aged 35 to 64 are projected to run short of money during retirement. This is based on a database of 27 million 401(k) participants and IRA account holders. This indicates that a whole lot of households are going to run short.

And we are all living longer: longevity may be one of the most dangerous factors in outliving our retirement savings. For couples aged 65 years, 50 percent will have one partner live past 92 years; and 25 percent will have one partner live past 96 years. That means one partner has a one in four chance of having to make it through thirty-one years of retirement.

———

Would it be a crazy thought that in approximately seven to nine years, you'd never have to make a mortgage payment again? Would it be a ridiculous idea that you could eliminate your debt while simultaneously building a tax-advantaged retirement plan?

———

We have all been taught that to build wealth, you must first pay off your debt. Is it possible to pay off debt while building a tax-advantaged retirement plan? What if I told you that you could eliminate your debt *and* build a tax-advantaged retirement plan at the same time? It may sound too good to be true, but it's not only possible, it's happening. Families like yours around the country are using the Money Max Pro Debt-to-Wealth System to eliminate their debt and simultaneously build wealth.

It seems too good to be true because what the banks have taught us about using money is too bad to believe.

SECTION 1:
DEBT AND THE U.S. DEBT CRISIS

EXPERTS FROM BOTH SIDES agree that we have a debt problem. It is one of the few situations Congress can agree on. Of course, they disagree on how to solve it. Why does this matter to American families?

The U.S. debt crisis refers to the growing national debt of the United States government, which has been increasing for several decades. As of 2023, the national debt is estimated to be over $33 trillion and expanding rapidly.

WHAT IS **THE NATIONAL DEBT** TODAY?

$33,691,906,174,870

That's

$100,678

for every single person in America.

More disturbing is the obligation rarely discussed by the geniuses in Washington, the unfunded liabilities.

Unfunded liabilities are future financial obligations of a government, company, or individual not currently backed by corresponding assets or funds to pay for them. For example, in a U.S. government context, unfunded liabilities could refer to promises made to fully fund school literacy programs that the government has not set aside enough funds to actually cover the costs.

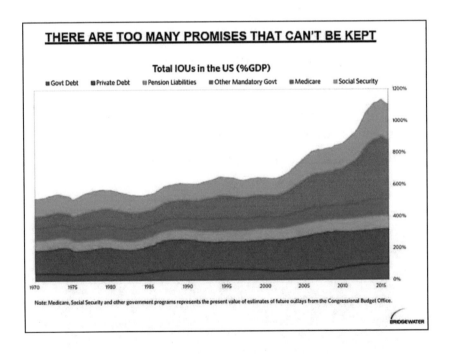

Unfunded liabilities can be a significant concern for a budget as they create a risk of future financial strain or bankruptcy for the entity responsible. In the case of a government, unfunded liabilities can burden future generations and limit the ability of the government to fund other essential priorities. To address unfunded liabilities, many experts recommend reducing future obligations, increasing funding for existing debts, or combining both. Unfunded U.S. liabilities are estimated to be $121 trillion and growing.

Sovereign Debt Crisis

The U.S. debt is the total financial obligation owed by the federal government. It is composed of:

- Public debt—reflected by U.S. Treasury notes
- Intragovernmental debt—what Treasury owes various government departments, the most considerable portion owed to Social Security
- **A sovereign debt** crisis is when a country cannot pay its bills. But this doesn't happen overnight; plenty of warning signs exist. It becomes a **crisis** when the country's leaders ignore these indicators for political reasons.

The United States holds the record for owning the most significant sovereign debt by a single country in the world. Because of its high debt-to-gross-domestic-product ratio, many worry about America's future ability to pay. In the debt ceiling negotiations by Congress and the White House, we can begin to see the dysfunction of our leadership. Even though they seemingly reach agreements, it is always short-term and just in the nick of time. What about next time? Is there any reason to think they will be better at this?

Let's Forget About It . . .

Have you ever watched the Wile E. Coyote cartoons where he is trying to outsmart the Road Runner? You may remember the episode where Wile E. has purchased an ACME Shed, and he is inside cutting the tops off of carrots (ACME carrots, of course) and filling them with explosives, all the while telling himself what a genius he is. In the meantime, unbeknownst to Wile E., the Road Runner has lassoed the shed and pulled it onto a railroad track. Wile E. goes about his work until he hears a train whistle. He stops, turns around, looks out the window, and sees a train bearing down on the shed. Does he get off the track? No, he pulls down the curtain. Of course, the train hits the shed and blows everything up, including Wile E., but he is no worse for the experience except for some burned fur.

We Americans are in the same boat. Our heads are stuck in the sand as we work to survive and hope to have a retirement before we die. Or is it OK to postpone dealing with this dynamite-filled shed a little longer?

Hope is not a strategy.

SECTION 2:
TAXES, TAXES, TAXES . . .

THROUGHOUT MY CAREER in financial planning, I taught classes for adult learners (lifetime learners) at two community colleges and one university. While discussing income taxes, I always asked my students, "Do you think taxes will go up, down, or stay the same?" I don't remember anyone ever answering, "Stay the same," or "Go down."

Your IRA or 401(k)—Tax Postponed Accounts

Remember when old movies showed retirement parties for people who, after working forty-five years at the company store, had reached that glorious day? The lucky guy's friends gathered around to congratulate him, and the big boss called him to the podium and handed him a small, gift-wrapped box. All his co-workers watched in eager silence because they knew they would one day be next to the boss as he gave them the small box. Our hero pulled the ribbon and carefully opened the gift—it was a gold watch! All that dedication and service, and *he* was the one getting the thanks.

He also received a company pension. It wasn't as much as he took home every month, but man, it was great to know that with the company pension and his Social Security, he could now retire and sit quietly on the porch after mowing his perfectly manicured lawn with a cold brew in his hand. Every month, *that* check arrived like clockwork. His hard work and dedication had paid off. He had made it.

Beginning with the advent of the 401(k) in 1980, also known as *Defined Contribution Plans,* and then the use of Mutual Funds in these retirement plans, the door for the average investor was kicked wide open. No longer able to count on a *Defined Benefit Plan* (pension) from their employer, the onus for a successful retirement was moved from the company to the individual, and its risks fell to the individual. Great for the companies but not so good for the employees. No more gold watches.

One of the most essential concepts of deferred contributions is that your IRA is yours alone. I've got some terrible news for you. You have a partner, and it's not your spouse. It's your Uncle Sam. He will determine and dictate when you pay the taxes on the IRA and how much you will pay. It is reported that bank robber Willie Sutton was asked, "Why do you rob banks?" He replied, "That's where the money is!" Your rich Uncle Sam looks at it the same way.

David Royer, the author of *Top Ten IRA Mistakes,* speaks to navigating the retirement maze. In addition to the above about taxes and the IRS, he also tells us that the second myth is that you can beat the tax. Your contract with the IRS cannot be broken. There is no "out clause." Even when you die, your uncle will get his share (your beneficiaries will be taxed). Again, the IRS will decide when you or your heirs will pay the tax and how much (percentage) will be taxed. Your uncle never loses or sleeps.

When you were hired, and the H.R. department shared with you some of the benefits of your coming to work for ACME, you were excited to find that they had a 401(k) plan. It looked great, and in many ways, it was. ACME would contribute or match up to 3 percent of your contribution, and that income you set aside for retirement would not be taxed as you saved; it would grow tax-deferred (postponed). It almost seemed too good to be true. And it was. Your favorite Uncle Sam would give you a break and not collect taxes on the money you set aside in your 401(k), nor would he tax you on the growth. But, what he didn't say was that you would not be taxed on the "seed," your 401(k) contributions. However, after tending to the "crop" (your employer contributions plus growth), when you began to draw down from it after you retired (the harvest) he would tax it at whatever rate he and Congress decided was in their best interest. If taxes were more when you retired than when you were working, you made a slight miscalculation.

Think about it like this. You want to borrow money for that boat you've dreamed of owning. You go to your local credit union and sit with a lender. You show her the boat pictures, the survey, and the sales price. You have 30 percent down (the boat is $100,000) and must finance the balance. The loan officer tells you your credit and the boat's value are also good. You are scheduled to have a closing over the weekend.

She says, "How would you like the funds: deposited in your account or a cashier's check?"

In your account will be fine, you tell her.

She says, "OK," and reaches out to shake your hand, and as she does so, she says, "I'll have my assistant draw up the loan documents."

You are ready to shake her hand, but you draw back. You think, *We never discussed interest rates or payback terms.* So, you hesitate, look up at her outstretched hand and into her eyes, and say, "Marsha, aren't we forgetting some details on this loan?"

She stops, looks directly at you, and asks, "What do you mean?"

You reply, "Well, what are the interest rate and term?" This is important.

She pulls back her hand, takes a deep breath, and replies, "Oh, those details. Well, let me share the terms of this loan with you."

You sit back in your seat and carefully watch her face. She says, "You have great credit; you've been a long-time customer of the bank; and we value your family and our relationship. We want to serve you, but we're just unsure about the rates right now. Tell you what, take the loan, and when we need the money back, we'll let you know the rate and terms."

What? No one would borrow that way. No one would have a partner without knowing what the costs are. But that's precisely what your IRA or 401(k) has done for you. You were a careful steward: you saved, you did without, you made sure your company had a match on the deferred accounts, and you carefully tended the "garden" of your finances. And now, you are looking forward to moving from the Accumulation phase into the Distribution phase for your retirement. You are ready to reap the benefits that your carefully considered and executed saving strategy accumulated. It's time to use this tax-deferred account to replace your paycheck.

But now, your partner, Uncle Sam, says, "I want my share."

It doesn't have to be this way.

SECTION 3:
UNITED FINANCIAL FREEDOM & UNITED FINANCIAL WEALTH

United Financial Freedom (UFF) and **United Financial Wealth (UFW)** are companies dedicated to helping you successfully eliminate your debt while simultaneously assisting you in building wealth for a genuinely safe and predictable retirement. UFF teaches you how to eliminate debt in the fastest mathematical way and shows you the cause and effect of your spending. UFW simultaneously builds wealth while eliminating your debt. When you combine UFF, the debt elimination system, with UFW, the wealth-building system, you are on track to achieve the most significant financial success you can accomplish.

Again, does it sound too good to be true? That's because the way the banks and financial sector are set up and how they have taught us to use money since we were young is *too bad to believe.*

United Financial Freedom (UFF)

Eliminating all your debt in one-third to half the time is a powerful strategy to free you from the continuous cycle of debt. Some of you may recall a tradition from long ago that is rarely seen in today's society—the mortgage burning party. At the end of the thirty-year mortgage, with the final payment made, the family and friends of a newly debt-free homeowner would gather for a campfire and celebration. All would cheer as the mortgage contract was tossed into the flames. Yahoo! The house was finally paid off.

Few of us remember these events because they rarely happen in today's mortgage structures. In 2021, twenty-five percent of mortgage holders refinanced. Low-interest rates and easy money have made refinancing or buying a new home a regular part of a family's routine. The banks love this. Because all mortgage loans (and most other loans) are front-end loaded, most interest comes out first, and the principal is slowly paid down.

If you were fortunate enough to have refinanced or purchased a home in the past few years, you might have a low-interest rate on that mortgage. A 3.5 percent 30-year fixed mortgage rate will see a payment of equal parts—principal and interest—at about payment number one hundred and twenty-three, or about ten years into the loan. If your interest rate on your mortgage was 3 percent, the payment where half went to interest and half to principal would occur at payment number eighty-four. If the loan rate was 4 percent, you would be waiting until payment number one hundred and fifty-four, about thirteen years after you began making payments to have *half* of that monthly payment go to the principal reduction. The other half would still go to interest. (For print readers, you can find up-to-date 30-year mortgage rates at hsh.com.)

In today's mortgage environment, with average rates on a new thirty-year fixed mortgage around 7.2 percent, if you refinance or purchase a new home today, you will not be at the mid-way point in that loan until 2043—an astounding 20.3 years. Do you think the banks are pretty happy about that?

Here's what a current mortgage would look like:

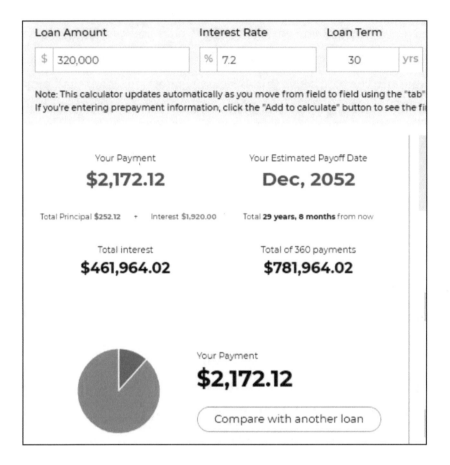

For an initial mortgage of $320,000, you will pay almost $462,000 in interest (bank profit) for a total of nearly $782,000! (Remember, it's too bad to believe.) Finally, if you keep the house that long, in 2042, you will still be paying more toward interest than principal on your monthly payment. It's just math! It's also why banks have the most prominent buildings in every town. They understand how to use money much more effectively than the general public. They keep cash moving constantly, never sitting, but always invested and earning.

Amortization Schedule

Year	Principal	Interest	Total Payment	Balance
⊕ 2023	$3,127.33	$22,938.14	$26,065.47	$316,872.67
⊕ 2024	$3,360.08	$22,705.39	$26,065.47	$313,512.59
⊕ 2025	$3,610.15	$22,455.32	$26,065.47	$309,902.44
⊕ 2026	$3,878.83	$22,186.63	$26,065.46	$306,023.60
⊕ 2027	$4,167.51	$21,897.95	$26,065.46	$301,856.09
⊕ 2028	$4,477.68	$21,587.79	$26,065.47	$297,378.41
⊕ 2029	$4,810.92	$21,254.54	$26,065.46	$292,567.49
⊕ 2030	$5,168.97	$20,896.49	$26,065.46	$287,398.51
⊕ 2031	$5,553.67	$20,511.80	$26,065.47	$281,844.84
⊕ 2032	$5,967.00	$20,098.47	$26,065.47	$275,877.84
⊕ 2033	$6,411.09	$19,654.38	$26,065.47	$269,466.76
⊕ 2034	$6,888.23	$19,177.24	$26,065.47	$262,578.53
⊕ 2035	$7,400.88	$18,664.59	$26,065.47	$255,177.65
⊕ 2036	$7,951.68	$18,113.79	$26,065.47	$247,225.97
⊕ 2037	$8,543.48	$17,521.99	$26,065.47	$238,682.50
⊕ 2038	$9,179.32	$16,886.15	$26,065.47	$229,503.18
⊕ 2039	$9,862.48	$16,202.98	$26,065.46	$219,640.69
⊕ 2040	$10,596.49	$15,468.98	$26,065.47	$209,044.20
⊕ 2041	$11,385.12	$14,680.34	$26,065.46	$197,659.08
⊕ 2042	$12,232.45	$13,833.01	$26,065.46	$185,426.63
⊕ 2043	$13,142.84	$12,922.62	$26,065.46	$172,283.78

The Money Max Account from UFF has turned the table on the banks and rewritten this script for thousands of families. Instead of never having that mortgage-burning party in thirty years, the average family will have *all* of their debt retired in as little as five to seven years *without* modifying their lifestyle. The strategy is not about scrimping and saving but emulating the bank's money strategy—using your money smarter and banking like the banks. Which would you rather be: the bank or the bank's customer?

Debt Analysis/Wealth Building

We at UFW are taking a new approach to eliminating debt and building a safe, dependable, tax-advantaged retirement. Our mission is to help you to identify the areas where you are *unknowingly* and *unnecessarily* transferring your hard-earned money to others and to help you to recognize and eliminate those losses.

One of our licensed agents will begin by asking you a few questions about your financial situation.

- **ABOUT YOU**—Your age, other accounts like 401(k) or IRAs, current insurance policies, when you want to retire, and what you would like your income to be when you retire.
- **INCOME**—When and how much are you paid?
- **BANK ACCOUNTS**—What do you typically have in your checking and savings accounts? We don't need any account numbers.
- **DEBT**—What debt do you have? We want to know about mortgages, credit cards, student loans, vehicles, or other obligations.
- **EXPENSES**—How much of your income goes to pay your bills and living expenses? How much discretionary income do you have (the money left after all your monthly debt and lifestyle expenses are paid)? *The system will only work if you have more income than your expenses, even with as little as a hundred dollars a month.*

Our *Financial GPS* analyzes your debt and finds the fastest way to eliminate that debt, using your money in the most efficient way possible.

Over the years, UFF has been honored with multiple accolades. We received the Ernst & Young Entrepreneur of the Year award in the financial services category for the Utah region and have been featured in multiple news stories, magazines, and newspaper articles. But the most rewarding recognition we received is from the individual home-owners who took a leap of faith and realized there is a better way to live than signing your financial lives away for thirty-plus years.

As of December 2023, with the program's assistance, thousands of homeowners and non-homeowners across the United States have eliminated *more than $2.4 billion* in debt and have $8.5 billion in debt under management in the Money Max Account program. Moreover, many of our clients are now entirely debt-free *and building wealth with the Money Max Pro Debt-to-Wealth System!*

WHAT THIS FINANCIAL METHOD IS

- This *IS* a proven way to eliminate debt quickly
- This *IS* a proven method to help consumers build wealth
- This financial method works with or without good credit *and* improves your credit

WHAT THIS FINANCIAL METHOD IS NOT

- This *IS NOT* a bi-weekly payment program or refinance
- This *IS NOT* an increase to your minimum monthly payments
- This *IS NOT* a mortgage modification, alteration, or any other change to your current mortgage

Who Can Benefit from This Strategy?

Anyone who has debt and makes more money than they spend.

We have found that the people who benefit the most from this strategy are those who are tired of making interest payments on their debt and are looking for a better way. People who would love to see what it is like to be debt-free and build wealth for life.

We would agree that the claim "Pay off your home in as little as five to seven years" sounds like a bold statement, but not only is it possible, in reality, thousands of homeowners all across the United States have been successfully implementing the financial methods of UFF since 2016.

"What?" you might be thinking. That's a lot to absorb. I'm happy to report debt reduction is just the first benefit. With the Money Max Pro Debt-to-Wealth System you can *build wealth* while eliminating debt!

Earlier in this booklet, I asked, "If what you thought you knew to be true turned out not to be, when would you want to know? Today? Tomorrow? Five years? Never?"

How about *now*?

You *can* have that gold watch.

United Financial Wealth—Building Wealth from Debt

What if you have already watched the Money Max Account videos and met with your UFF agent? They ran an analysis for your debt elimination strategy, and you have begun to understand how your world will change when you utilize your money the same way the banks do. You already understand that using the Money Max Pro debt elimination software will free you sooner from debt.

The next step is the **Money Max Pro Debt-to-Wealth System**.

When we show this strategy to families, I often hear, "This seems too good to be true." Again, I reply, "That's because the little bit of learning we have received over the years about money is too bad to believe." *Everything* works in favor of the banks and financial planners.

My wife is a physician. She jokes that she completed grade twenty-three. She has a lot of education. Yet, throughout the challenging courses in pursuit of her M.D., she can only remember one study about personal finance and financial well-being.

No matter what your occupation or training: engineer, mechanic, physician, or teacher, we learn to assess a situation and make decisions based on fact and logic. Yet, regarding money, our strategy is often based on emotion and sales pressure.

What's a four-letter word that is not emotional nor changes with time? **Math.**

Math is the four-letter word to which we should all be paying attention.

The Money Max Pro Debt-to-Wealth System will guide and assist you in making decisions based on fact, logic, and math to eliminate debt and *simultaneously* put you on the path to building a tax-advantaged and predictable retirement fund. Think of it as your private pension.

How's it done? By adding a high-cash-value permanent life insurance policy—a proven financial instrument—to what you are already doing with the Money Max Account.

With the UFF Money Max Account, you focus on using the "third account"—checking, savings, credit cards, or a HELOC (home equity line of credit)—as the intelligent way to utilize money more efficiently and eliminate your debt in one-third to one-half the time. Your thirty-year mortgage and *all* of your debt are eliminated without sacrificing your lifestyle.

Imagine: With UFW's Money Max Pro Debt-to-Wealth Building System, what if that "third account" could use your money even more efficiently *and* build a retirement account *while* paying off your debt? That is precisely what the Money Max Pro Debt-to-Wealth Building System will do for you by using a high-cash-value permanent life insurance policy. You see, a properly constructed high-cash-value permanent life insurance policy can be used as a savings or investment vehicle through certain types of policies, such as whole life insurance or indexed universal life insurance

(IUL), and also provide a death benefit to beneficiaries in the event of the policyholder's death. These policies accumulate cash value over time, which can be *borrowed against*, used to pay premiums, or cashed out. It can never go down in value except by your withdrawals. The Money Max Pro Debt-to-Wealth Building system will utilize this cash "savings" account within your IUL to first grow and then pay off debt (approximately 80-90% of the premium you pay will be available for loans). The accumulation value of the account will continue to grow based upon the interest accrued. *That* is a pretty big claim. Let's look at how a properly constructed permanent life insurance policy works.

You can watch The Money Max Pro Debt-to-Wealth System Video here if you are reading this in an electric format, or go to this URL – https://vimeo.com/815141783/2ebb45803a

How Permanent High Cash Value Life Insurance Works:

Bank Like the Bank

Let's say you have a savings account at your local bank, People's United Savings, and the bank pays you 2 percent interest on that balance. It doesn't add up to much, but you are relieved to know the money is safe and getting some return.

Imagine you have $100,000 in your bank savings account. To buy a new bass boat, you withdraw $35,000, leaving a balance of $65,000. Your friends at the bank will now pay you that great 2 percent interest on the account's balance.

But what if you had a way to borrow the money from yourself *and still earn interest as though you'd never taken any money from that account?* And what if the typical interest rate on that account averaged about 6 to 7 percent?

"Not possible," you'd say.

Well, it is the way the wealthy and those who understand the "Bank on Yourself" strategies have been building wealth for years and years. Even when you withdraw money from that specialized account to buy something or pay off debt, that account continues to grow on the entire principal as though you had never withdrawn any money. You are "double dipping," you are doing what is known as leveraging—using the same money twice.

Traditionally, financial leverage is an investment strategy of using borrowed money with the goal of reaping a greater return than the cost of borrowing the funds.

For example, real estate investors are often highly leveraged in the traditional financial sense. They may purchase many investment properties, build equity in the properties, and use that equity to buy more homes. We know that this type of real estate investing can have risks, like what happened in the mortgage meltdown in 2007–2008. After almost unrealistic growth in those properties, it all came crashing down, with many properties losing 30 to 40 percent of their value in a very short time.

When using a life insurance policy for leveraging, you are borrowing money *from your policy (i.e. on yourself) not from the bank.* The death benefit collateralizes the loan from your insurance policy: at your death, the amount of the loan you took plus any interest accrued is deducted from the proceeds of the death benefit payment if the loan has not yet been repaid. You can choose to repay the loan or not. In a properly designed permanent life insurance policy, the interest rate earned is greater than the internal interest rate charged on the loans. This creates a positive arbitrage—the spread between the two. For example, with an internal loan rate of 5 percent and the policy averaging 6 percent, you have a positive arbitrage of 1 percent. Over time, this is very powerful.

Unlike real estate leverage, with the risk of being "upside down" in the investment (owing more on the property than it is worth), UFW advocates for the use of financial leverage in your retirement plan that does *not* increase—and in most cases *decreases*—the amount of risk in your portfolio. It's a powerful way to make your money work for you in two ways.

Let me explain. (See Appendix 1 for the full explanation of the IUL.)

In a properly designed permanent life insurance policy, there are three values:

1. Cash value or surrender value—in an indexed universal life insurance policy, the cash value growth is linked to the performance of a specific stock market index, such as the S&P 500, PIMCO, Blackrock, or others. It is never actually in the markets. This is called indexing. The indexing strategy determines how the cash value is credited to the account based on the movement, up or down, of the chosen index. If those indices have a positive year, the cash value in your account will go up. But, in an IUL policy, if the indices linked to that account have a negative return, your account does not go down. The cash value (also known as the surrender value) of the IUL policy can only go down if you make a withdrawal, either as a loan or by using the cash value to pay the premiums on the IUL. Your account can *never* decrease in value from a bad year in the markets.

2. Accumulation value—The accumulation value of a life in-surance policy refers to the amount of money accumulated or grown over time within the policy. It represents the policy's total value, including the premiums paid by the policyholder, any interest or investment gains, and the deduction of any fees or charges. In a properly designed permanent life insurance policy, the accumulation value can only increase or stay the same. Pay careful attention to the following sentence—this is one of the most important concepts to understand. *Even when you withdraw from the cash value of the policy, the accumulated value continues to go up with dividends or the interest it earns.*

3. Death benefit—The death benefit in an IUL insurance poli-cy refers to the amount of money paid to the beneficiaries upon the insured's death. It is an essential purpose of life insurance and provides financial protection to the policyholder's loved ones in the event of the policyholder's death.

Understanding why the Money Max Account Pro Wealth Building Strategy works with a permanent life insurance policy as the third account is critical. Even when you withdraw from the cash value of your policy—for example, to pay down on debt—the accumulation value of your policy continues to grow. It does not go down in value. Remember the savings account you withdrew the money from to pay for the boat? That account continued to pay interest but only on $65,000, not the whole $100,000. When you borrow from your IUL policy to pay down debt or purchase something, the accumulation value of the policy continues to grow as though you did not make any withdrawals.

Once you understand how this vital part of properly constructed life insurance works, you will begin to see why we can utilize this strategy to pay down debt and build a future tax-advantaged income for retirement. You will build wealth while simultaneously eliminating your debt.

What is the average rate of return in an Indexed Universal Life Insurance Policy?

A minimum percentage return is guaranteed on an IUL with the possibility of returns between 8 to12 percent. This may make IUL more attractive as an investment than whole life insurance, which earns a lower rate of return.

The Money Max Pro Debt-to-Wealth System has researched hundreds of the best permanent life insurance policies available. We have tested them for several important factors critical to the maximum performance of the Money Max Pro Debt-to-Wealth System:

1. Strength of the company and historical performance

2. Non-direct recognition—meaning the policy's accumulated value grows regardless of loans

3. Low surrender value in year one—what we call early liquidity

4. Flexibility for loans—can withdraw in year one if necessary

5. Maximize growth after debt elimination to create a private pension fund for retirement

6. Tax-deferred growth and tax-advantaged withdrawals (in the form of loans)

After putting numerous companies and their policies to the test, one stood out above the rest and met all the requirements to maximize debt elimination and build wealth.

In more than 173 years, this company has insured everyone from celebrities to working people, including passengers on the Titanic and the Hindenburg and victims of the great influenza epidemic of 1918–1919. The Vermont Legislature chartered this company on November 13, 1848. Here is how the three rating companies assess them:

A.M. BEST		STANDARD & POOR'S		MOODY'S	
A++	(Superior)	AAA (Extremely Strong)		Aaa	(Exceptional)
		AA+	(Very Strong)	Aa1	(Excellent)
A+**	(Superior)	AA	(Very Strong)	Aa2	(Excellent)
		AA-	(Very Strong)	Aa3	(Excellent)
A	(Excellent)	A+**	(Strong)	A1**	(Good)
		A	(Strong)	A2	(Good)
A-	(Excellent)	A-	(Strong)	A3	(Good)

A detailed look at the IUL use in this strategy can be found in Appendix 1.

Putting Things Together

Now that you understand the benefits of utilizing permanent life insurance as a financial strategy let's look at how the Money Max Pro Debt-to-Wealth System eliminates debt even more efficiently than just having the UFF Money Max Account.

As we shared earlier in this booklet, the Money Max Account system will act as a financial GPS to find the fastest and most efficient way to eliminate your debt. John Lennon once wrote, "Life is what happens when you're busy making other plans."

As you increase your income, have unanticipated expenses, or any of the other changes life will bring, the program adjusts and finds the path to financial freedom most efficiently. When you add the *UFW Money Max Account Pro Debt-to-Wealth System* to your UFF Money Max Account plan, it takes your debt and wealth strategy to another level. Best of all, ***there is no additional charge to upgrade to this powerful system.***

While you and the program concentrate on eliminating your debt most efficiently, you are simultaneously building a tax-advantaged retirement plan.

Watch this video now to understand this tool's simple complexity: - Money Max Pro Debt-to-Wealth System Video. (If you are reading the print version of this book, you can search for the Interest Cancellation video on the United Financial Freedom YouTube page.)

The Money Max Pro will build your wealth in the background as you continue eliminating your debt through the Money Max Pro Debt-to-Wealth System strategies. It's so simple that you will say, why didn't I think of this?

31

SECTION 4: CASE STUDIES

Case Study I: John & Rebecca Jones

Bob and Catherine Palmer are a typical family. They heard about the Money Max Pro Debt-to-Wealth System from their friends, John Jones and his wife Rebecca, who began using it a couple of years ago. They were curious when their friends shared that after only two years of using the system, they had paid off several of their loans and made some significant dents in others. They were on track to be out of debt entirely in five more years.

The Palmers and the Joneses have a monthly backyard barbecue get-together in the spring and summer. Over steaks and corn on the cob, John shared with Bob and Catherine that they were not only on track to get out of debt in 9.1 years, but upon retirement, they would have a private pension fund of approximately $126,000 a year or about $10,000 a month for twenty-five years! And it would all be tax-advantaged! There was no skimping or extra saving; their lifestyle would remain the same. As they eliminated their debt, their wealth would begin building simultaneously.

To the Palmers, this financial paradise was likely a false hope masquerading as reality. Bob and Catherine were always skeptical—they were from Missouri, the Show Me State, and followed the code, "if something seemed too good to be true, it probably was." Maybe the beer, the steaks, and the intoxicating night stars had tipped John from exuberance to downright exaggeration.

Rebecca, the conservative, careful counterpart to John's enthusiastic ways, suggested they meet again next weekend over iced tea, not beer, and revisit the discussion.

Iced Tea and a Pastry

Over the next several days, Catherine reflected on their discussion as she sat in her home office. She took care of the family finances and paid the mortgage and the student loans she and Bob had accrued to get into their excellent university. She ran the numbers for money they could safely spend on the next seaside vacation. She wanted to make sure their two kids grew up with the same fun family memories she'd had as a kid. No matter how she ran the numbers or how carefully they spent, their debt seemed almost like it would never be paid off. She knew their current home, as great as it was, would be too small if they had another child, and the debt cycle would continue.

John's financial claims seemed impossible. She'd taken some college accounting courses, and math was math. John and Rebecca would not only be debt-free twenty years *before* she and Bob would be, but John said they would have a tax-advantaged income for thirty years in the six-figure range.

It had to be the beer talking.

Kids, soccer practice, homework, and the work of running the household made the week go by swiftly, and she awakened a little bit more than curious on Saturday morning. She would bring fresh cinnamon rolls. She was excited to see this miracle of math . . . and to find the holes.

It Is Just Math

After the usual pleasantries, everyone sat down in the Jones's den in front of a large screen John had fixed so everyone could easily see what his computer was showing.

Rebecca brought up their Money Max account on the screen, the dashboard showing their accounts, budget, years to pay off, and the payoff date.

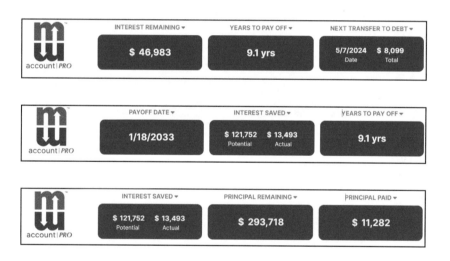

All of their living expenses were on the screen and Rebecca shared with them that when the inevitable event occurred—like the expense for a new roof or that dream vacation—the Money

Max Account (a Financial GPS) considered everything, adjusted the numbers, and found the fastest way to zero. Rebecca said she was pretty good with numbers, but this put everything on steroids, took the worry out of unexpected expenses, and kept them on track. It was like having a team of CPAs working for them.

The Money Max account directed every account and every transfer. All Rebecca had to do was log on and follow the prompts. Their next payment towards eliminating their debt and paying down the principal would be on 5/7/24 for $8,099 exactly. She didn't have to calculate or guess. The algorithms did the math for her. Once the cash value in the IUL has grown enough to make a transfer to pay towards debt elimination safely, the program will prompt her for the date and amount to pay.

The Personalized Savings Report

They would pay off $368,800 in debt in 9.1 years, and instead of paying the exorbitant profit to the bank (interest), they would save $124,419.

Your Personalized Savings Report

| For: John Jones II (age 39) | Debt-Free Goal: | Prepared By: Jason Ingram | Page 1 |
| 7757272@gmail.com | Jul 2049 | jason@jingramconsulting.com / (352) 871-3162 | Fri Dec 15, 2023 |

Summary of Debts

Name	Balance	Rate	Payment
Mortgage Debt (1)	$305,000.00	3.25%	$1,722.38
Loans (4)	$55,800.00	6.05%	$1,767.31
Credit Cards (1)	$8,000.00	18.00%	$203.04
Total	$368,800.00	3.99%	$3,692.73

Monthly Discretionary Income Analysis

Description	Amount	% of Income
Base Monthly Income	$7,700.00	100.0%
Monthly Debt Payments	$3,692.73	48.0%
Other Monthly Expenses	$3,382.27	43.9%
Index Universal Life Expense	$232.00	3.0%
Actual Premium Transfer	*$405.00*	*5.3%*
Term	*$96.41*	*1.3%*
Discretionary Income including IUL Expense	$296.59	3.9%
Discretionary Income including IUL Premium	*$123.59*	*1.6%*

Having debt is no walk in the park!

This month you'll pay *over $1,200 in interest alone*. That's 37% of your monthly payment ...*gone!*

On average over the next *30.0 years* your bank's plan will cost you *more than $500 per month* in interest.

You'll spend *$2.65 for every $1* you pay down in principal on your mortgage this month.

It will be *June 2039* (when you are *54 years old*) before you have paid off *half* of your debt and you will still owe *over $184,000.*

What The Money Max Account Pro can do for you

Your Bank's Plan	VS	The Money Max Account Pro	=	You Save
Total Debt Payments				
$559,767	vs	**$435,348**	=	**$124,419**
That's 52% more than your current outstanding balance of $368,800!		This is the total amount you will pay to completely eliminate all of your listed debts.		That's a BIG TIP for the bank! Let's make it 109 payments of $1,141.
Total Interest Payments				
$190,967	vs	**$66,548**	=	**$124,419**
That's 2.1 years worth of your entire income of $7,700/month just to cover the interest!		You would need an interest rate of 1.14% to pay this little interest on a new 30-year loan!		Save 65% in interest or 16 months worth of your entire income!
Projected Payoff				
30.0 years	vs	**9.1 years**	=	**20.9 years**
With 360 payments to go you'll still be making payments when you are 69 years old!		You'll be debt-free by age 47 after only 109 payments.		What could you do with 251 months with NO monthly debt payments?
Wealth Accumulation				
$0	vs	**$1,273,703**	=	**$1,273,703**
You'll be making debt payments for the next 30 years instead of building wealth.		With The Money Max Account Pro, we'll use your 20.9 years saved to start building wealth!		This is your savings with a 1% return. Imagine your savings at higher rates!

Why wait? Start saving today!

By getting started today you can save *over $124,000* in interest payments over the next 9.1 years.

By saving *20.9 years* of debt payments you could build *more than $1,273,000* in wealth over that same time period!

Each month you delay getting started will cost you *$1,141* on average over the next 9.1 years! *Don't wait! Start now!*

Debt-Free In	Debt-Free By	Years Saved	Total Savings	Avg. Savings/Mo
9.1 years	Dec-2032	20.9	$124,419	$1,141

The chart showed an amortization table of the loans (debt), and by the end of year eight, they would no longer be paying all this profit to the bank but could begin saving that interest to build their wealth.

Debt free in 9.1 years!

Your Personalized Savings Report

For: John Jones II (age 39) 7757272@gmail.com	Debt-Free Goal: Jul 2049	Prepared By: Jason Ingram jason@ingramconsulting.com / (352) 871-3162		Page 2 Fri Dec 15, 2023

Amortization and Wealth Accumulation Schedule

Year	Age	Issue Age	Balance As Scheduled	Balance with Our Program
today	39	40	($368,800.00)	($372,595.00)
1 (2024)	40	41	($343,411.29)	($343,411.30)
2 (2025)	41	42	($321,986.10)	($321,986.10)
3 (2026)	42	43	($306,880.42)	($278,393.64)
4 (2027)	43	44	($293,932.27)	($237,460.42)
5 (2028)	44	45	($280,458.41)	($194,169.73)
6 (2029)	45	46	($266,874.20)	($149,023.47)
7 (2030)	46	47	($251,007.91)	($102,387.91)
8 (2031)	47	48	($252,951.29)	($54,213.90)
9 (2032)	48	49	($244,689.64)	($4,450.70)
10 (2033)	49	50	($236,208.79)	$50,418.09
11 (2034)	50	51	($227,495.02)	$105,949.09
12 (2035)	51	52	($218,534.95)	$162,037.95
13 (2036)	52	53	($209,315.44)	$218,690.28
14 (2037)	53	54	($199,823.52)	$275,911.73
15 (2038)	54	55	($190,046.36)	$333,708.03
16 (2039)	55	56	($179,971.14)	$392,084.95
17 (2040)	56	57	($169,585.06)	$451,048.32
18 (2041)	57	58	($158,875.23)	$510,604.03
19 (2042)	58	59	($147,828.69)	$570,758.04
20 (2043)	59	60	($136,432.30)	$631,516.35
21 (2044)	60	61	($124,665.68)	$692,885.04
22 (2045)	61	62	($112,498.52)	$754,870.24
23 (2046)	62	63	($99,914.81)	$817,478.14
24 (2047)	63	64	($86,897.49)	$880,714.99
25 (2048)	64	65	($73,428.76)	$944,587.12
26 (2049)	65	66	($59,670.57)	$1,009,100.91
27 (2050)	66	67	($45,471.03)	$1,074,262.79
28 (2051)	67	68	($30,803.06)	$1,140,079.30
30 (Nov 2053)	69	69	$0.00	$1,273,702.51

Debts to be Paid Off

Name	Balance	Rate	Payment
Mortgage	$305,000.00	3.25%	$1,722.38
Student Loan	$30,000.00	6.70%	$535.00
Truck Loan	$15,000.00	3.75%	$543.60
Discover Card	$8,000.00	18.00%	$203.04
Yamaha Motorcycle	$6,000.00	10.00%	$318.71
Car Loan	$4,800.00	4.25%	$370.00
Total	$368,800.00	3.99%	$3,692.73

"Those who don't understand interest are doomed to pay it...

...Those who do are destined to earn it."

- Author Unknown

Debt-Free In	Debt-Free By	Years Saved	Total Savings	Avg. Savings/Mo
9.1 years	Dec-2032	20.9	$124,419	$1,141

Rebecca had learned about the Money Max Account and UFF from a friend. Like Catherine and Bob, Rebecca had also thought it sounded like a pipe dream at first, but using the system for the last couple of years had erased any doubts. She explained they had been using the Money Max Account for two years when their agent met with them and shared the latest free upgrade from the folks at UFF, the Money Max Account Pro.

Then, she demonstrated what happened when they upgraded their Money Max Account to the Money Max Pro Debt-to-Wealth System.

With this free upgrade, the Joneses were on track to not only pay off their debt in 9.1 years but save $124,419 in interest that would have gone to the banks but now would give them a predictable income at their retirement of about $118,728 a year for thirty years. She shared with them an overview of their system's results.

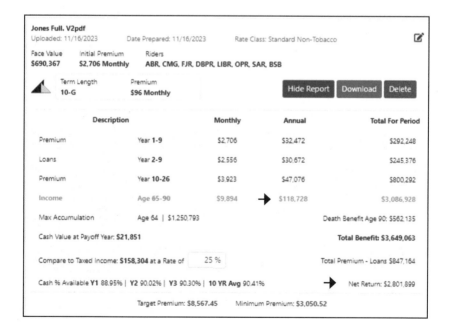

Jones Full. V2pdf
Uploaded: 11/16/2023   Date Prepared: 11/16/2023   Rate Class: Standard Non-Tobacco

Face Value   Initial Premium   Riders
$690,367 $2,706 Monthly   ABR, CMG, FJR, DBPR, LIBR, OPR, SAR, BSB

Term Length   Premium
10-G $96 Monthly   [Hide Report] [Download] [Delete]

Description		Monthly	Annual	Total For Period
Premium	Year 1-9	$2,706	$32,472	$292,248
Loans	Year 2-9	$2,556	$30,672	$245,376
Premium	Year 10-26	$3,923	$47,076	$800,292
Income	Age 65-90	$9,894	→ $118,728	$3,086,928

Max Accumulation   Age 64 | $1,250,793   Death Benefit Age 90: $562,135

Cash Value at Payoff Year: $21,851   Total Benefit: $3,649,063

Compare to Taxed Income: $158,304 at a Rate of 25 %   Total Premium - Loans $847,164

Cash % Available Y1 88.95% | Y2 90.02% | Y3 90.30% | 10 YR Avg 90.41%   → Net Return: $2,801,899

Target Premium: $8,567.45   Minimum Premium: $3,050.52

This chart showed that after using the Money Max Pro Debt-to-Wealth System, at age sixty-five, John and Rebecca will have a projected Accumulated Value in the life policy of $1,250,793 (which continues to earn interest), will have paid off debt of $368,000, and a projected income of $9,898 a month ($118,728/year) from age sixty-five to ninety years. And, when John died (projected age 90), he would leave $562,135 (projected) to his beneficiaries if he lived into his 90s.

In a Safehome.org 2022 survey of America's top ten fears, "Loved ones becoming seriously ill, high medical bills, becoming terminally ill, and not having enough money for retirement" topped the list.

With the Money Max Pro Debt-to-Wealth System, living benefits are included in the IUL policy. Free riders on the policy include protection from Terminal Illness, Chronic Illness, Critical Injury, Critical Illness, and Alzheimer's Disease.

Additional Benefits

Protect your retirement plan with living benefits from your Indexed Universal Life and Term life.

Terminal Illness	Chronic Illness	
$1,657,012	**$15,722**	
Combined Lump Sum Payout	Combined Monthly Payout	

Critical Illness	Critical Injury	Alzheimer's Disease
$1,495,888	**$1,495,888**	**$1,149,866**
Combined Lump Sum Payout	Combined Lump Sum Payout	Combined Lump Sum Payout

Rebecca's enthusiasm was contagious. It wasn't hocus pocus; it was just having a partner (the Money Max Pro Debt-to-Wealth System) who would help them stay on track, eliminate their debt most efficiently, simultaneously build wealth, and provide extended care should they need it.

Catherine thought, "How will this work for us?" What if they could not only be out from under the yoke of debt but also relax knowing they would have a high income in retirement? They didn't need a gold watch. They had something way better.

After a lively discussion followed by the iced tea and pastries, Rebecca promised she would introduce the Palmers to their UFF agent on Monday.

Case Study II: Dr. Paula Roberts

Dr. Paula Roberts is a forty-year-old physician, married to Jan. Their combined debt includes a mortgage, medical school loans, a car, and a few small credit cards, which add up to $680,000 in total. Paula and her partner have a combined income of $20,300 and living expenses of $12,000 monthly. Their discretionary income is around $2,300/month.

Type	Name	Balance	Rate	Remaining		Payment
	M&T - Primary	$320,000	3.541 %	30.0-years	→	$1,669
	Sallie Mae	$315,000	5.250 %	10.0-years		$3,380
	Toyota 4 Runner	$35,000	4.000 %	5.0-years		$645
	BofA Visa	$10,000	18.000 %	n/a		$250
	All Debts	$680,000	4.569 %	30.0-years		$5,944

Name	Amount	Frequency	*Base Monthly	...
Monthly Expenses	$12,000	Monthly	$12,000	
Income			$20,230	
Expenses		-	$12,000	
Debt Payments		-	$5,944	
Discretionary Income		=	$2,286	

Yes, they were aware of paying off debt with extra payments here or there, but it seemed that life always got in the way, and their efforts were sporadic. They kept thinking they would pay off some of the debt if they both received bonuses. Their student loans were particularly discouraging. It seemed like they would die owing Sallie Mae.

And it seemed like they were always short at the end of the month to put anything toward reducing their debt. She had recently read an article that identified their problem: Parkinson's Law—expenses always rise to meet income. The couple's intentions were good, but life got in the way.

If only they had a partner to help them stay on task. Happily, they do.

An analysis of their situation utilizing the Money Max Pro Debt-to-Wealth System shows they will be debt-free in 7.1 years with total interest savings of $203,411.

Your Personalized Savings Report

For: **Dr.Paula Roberts** (age 35)
paula@gmai.com

Debt-Free Goal:
Mar 2033

Prepared By: **Jason Ingram**
jason@jingramconsulting.com / (352) 871-3162

Page 1
Sun May 28. 2023

Summary of Debts

Name	Balance	Rate	Payment
Mortgage Debt (1)	$320,000.00	3.54%	$1,669.28
Loans (2)	$350,000.00	5.13%	$4,024.27
Credit Cards (1)	$10,000.00	18.00%	$250.00
Total	**$680,000.00**	**4.57%**	**$5,943.55**

Discretionary Income Analysis

Description	Amount	% of Income
Base Monthly Income	$20,230.00	100.0%
Monthly Debt Payments	$5,943.55	29.4%
Other Monthly Expenses	$12,000.00	59.3%
Term	$217.40	1.1%
Monthly Discretionary Income	**$2,286.45**	**11.3%**

Having debt is no walk in the park!

This month you'll pay *over $2,500 in interest alone*. That's *45%* of your monthly payment ...*gone!*

You'll spend *$2.89* for every *$1* you pay down in principal on your mortgage this month.

On average over the next *30.0 years* your bank's plan will cost you *more than $850 per month* in interest.

It will be *June 2031* (when you are *43 years old*) before you have paid off *half* of your debt and you will still owe *over $337,000.*

What The Money Max Account Pro can do for you

Your Bank's Plan	vs	The Money Max Account Pro	=	You Save
Total Debt Payments				
$986,818 — That's 45% more than your current outstanding balance of $680,000!	vs	**$783,407** — This is the total amount you will pay to completely eliminate all of your listed debts.	=	**$203,411** — That's a BIG TIP for the bank! Let's make it 85 payments of $2,393.
Total Interest Payments				
$306,818 — That's 15 months worth of your entire income of $20,230/month just to cover the interest!	vs	**$103,407** — You would need an interest rate of 0.96% to pay this little interest on a new 30-year loan!	=	**$203,411** — Save 66% in interest or 10 months worth of your entire income!
Projected Payoff				
30.0 years — With 360 payments to go you'll still be making payments when you are 65 years old!	vs	**7.1 years** — You'll be debt-free by age 42 after only 85 payments.	=	**22.9 years** — What could you do with 275 months with NO monthly debt payments?
Wealth Accumulation				
$0 — You'll be making debt payments for the next 30 years instead of building wealth	vs	**$2,839,213** — With The Money Max Account Pro, we'll use your 22.9 years saved to start building wealth!	=	**$2,839,213** — This is your savings with a 1% return. Imagine your savings at higher rates!

Why wait? Start saving today!

By getting started today you can save *over $203,000* in interest payments over the next 7.1 years.

By saving 22.9 years of debt payments you could build *more than $2,839,000* in wealth over that same time period!

Each month you delay getting started will cost you *$2,393* on average over the next 7.1 years! *Don't wait! Start now!*

Debt-Free In	Debt-Free By	Years Saved	Total Savings	Avg. Savings/Mo
7.1 years	May-2030	22.9	$203,411	$2,393

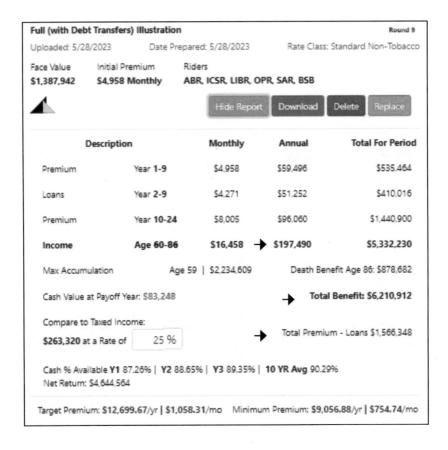

Full (with Debt Transfers) Illustration   Round 9

Uploaded: 5/28/2023   Date Prepared: 5/28/2023   Rate Class: Standard Non-Tobacco

Face Value	Initial Premium	Riders
$1,387,942	$4,958 Monthly	ABR, ICSR, LIBR, OPR, SAR, BSB

Hide Report   Download   Delete   Replace

Description		Monthly	Annual	Total For Period
Premium	Year 1-9	$4,958	$59,496	$535,464
Loans	Year 2-9	$4,271	$51,252	$410,016
Premium	Year 10-24	$8,005	$96,060	$1,440,900
Income	Age 60-86	$16,458 →	$197,490	$5,332,230

Max Accumulation   Age 59 | $2,234,609   Death Benefit Age 86: $878,682

Cash Value at Payoff Year: $83,248   → **Total Benefit: $6,210,912**

Compare to Taxed Income:

$263,320 at a Rate of   25 %   → Total Premium - Loans $1,566,348

Cash % Available **Y1** 87.26% | **Y2** 88.65% | **Y3** 89.35% | **10 YR Avg** 90.29%
Net Return: $4,644,564

Target Premium: $12,699.67/yr | $1,058.31/mo   Minimum Premium: $9,056.88/yr | $754.74/mo

With Paula and Jan's busy work lives and two kids, there was no time to "do it themselves," even if they could have the discipline. They found the perfect partner they were looking for—a Financial GPS—the Money Max Pro Debt-to-Wealth Building System.

Their Personalized Savings Report, prepared by a licensed UFW agent was truly astounding. (Talk to the agent who gave you this booklet, and she will run a free analysis for you.) Physicians face burnout more and more yearly. Paula wanted to retire as early as she was able. After medical school sacrifices, there was so much she had missed.

Unlock Your True Financial Potential

Our Wealth Builder System unlocks your true financial potential by strategically paying off debt and simultaneously building wealth.

Build Wealth After Eliminating Debt

Phase 2

	Monthly Until Age 60	Accumulated Value at Age 59
Proposed Wealth Building Account Plan:	$8,005	$3,298,787

	Monthly	Annually
Receive tax-advantaged income beginning at age 60 until age 86.	$16,458	$197,490

Tax-advantaged Net Death Benefit	Tax-advantaged Net Death Benefit	Income + Net Death Benefit
$3,941,075	**$878,682**	**$6,210,912**
At Age 59	At Age 86	Total Tax-advantaged at Age 86

By utilizing the Money Max Pro Debt-to-Wealth Building System, Paula would realize a projected accumulated value of her policy of $3,298,787 at age fifty-nine *after* eliminating $680,000 in debt. Her private pension fund was projected to be $197,490 a year in tax-advantaged income for twenty-five years, leaving her family a death benefit of approximately $878,682 at her life expectancy of eighty-five. Total income and Net Death Benefit would be roughly $6,210,912. Additionally, her Living Benefits looked like this.

According to the National Institute on Aging, long-term care is a broad term that describes various services and support for those who can no longer care for themselves due to age-related impairments.

As a physician, Paula had seen more horror stories around extended care than she could recall. Families upended their financial futures, all because a loved one needed long-term care. She hoped she would not need these services and that one day, she would go to bed and not wake up the next day. But the reality is different.

The **Living Benefits** of her wealth-building permanent life insurance policy were reassuring. She did not want to be a burden to her kids or to anyone else. She felt assured the money would be there if she needed this care as she aged. She was protected against chronic illness, critical injury, and Alzheimer's disease.

Advanced Strategies

Now that you've seen the power of the Money Max Pro Debt-to-Wealth Building System to both eliminate your debt and save you up to hundreds of thousands in profit that banks make on your loans, are you ready for an advanced strategy that will accelerate your debt elimination, and build a second "private pension" fund for your retirement?

The days of most Americans working for the same company for their careers are a thing of the past. Companies change, we get restless, and we move. According to the U.S. Bureau of Labor Statistics, the average salaried employee will have a tenure of 4.1 years for men and 3.9 for women. The segment of workers aged twenty-five to thirty-four-years-old averaged just 2.8 years in a role before transitioning to a new company or position. Meanwhile, senior workers between fifty-five and sixty-four years spend more than three times as long in a position, with an average median tenure of 9.9 years.

According to the job search service Indeed Career Guide, the top reasons we move from one job to another are:

1. Flexibility

2. Recognition

3. Higher pay

4. Feedback

5. More resources

6. Challenge

7. Effective management

8. Job satisfaction

9. Work-life balance

10. Benefits

The bottom line is that we Americans are changing jobs a lot more than we used to.

A study by the **Plan Sponsor Council of America** showed that 98 percent of companies that offer a 401(k) also provide employer matching for their employees. In employer-matched 401(k) plans, employers will contribute up to a specified amount. You can think of it as a bonus on top of your salary.

While most 401(k) plans are not accessible except for loans before the age of fifty-nine and half years without a 10 percent IRS penalty for withdrawals, there is a little-utilized exception to that regulation, known as IRS Code 72(t). When used correctly, this regulation will allow those withdrawals to assist in the funding of your Money Max Pro Debt-to-Wealth System.

How does Rule 72(t) work?

Internal Revenue Code section 72(t) allows penalty-free access to assets in IRAs and employer-sponsored retirement plans under certain conditions, such as account holder death or disability, first-time home purchases, and *taking substantially equal periodic payments.*

At UFW, we are utilizing a strategy for our eligible clients to eliminate their debt quicker, build their wealth account, *and* create another fund for their retirement by taking advantage of this IRS code, 72(t).

Market Risk

Risk: The potential for harm or financial loss

In 2001–2002 and again in 2007–2008, most investors lost 30 to 40 percent of their 401(k)s funds. When the market crashes, most qualified retirement plans like IRAs and 401(k)s crash. Even minor downturns can cause stress immediately before and after you retire. The markets always return, but what if you could stay ahead of the game? What if you *never* suffered a principal loss and only experienced the gain? It would be like if you were at a casino and could never lose when the roulette wheel turned. You could only win each spin of the wheel or take back your bet. The chips you held would never decrease. The pile would just grow or stay the same. That would make gambling a lot more fun. That will never happen in Las Vegas, but it can happen in your retirement accounts. No principal losses, only gains or zero.

We've already shared with you how a properly constructed IUL Permanent Life Insurance policy has little to no downside. The floor, or the worst it can do in any given year, is zero, and over the past twenty-five years, these policies have averaged far better. In fact, the Compound Average Growth Rate (CAGR) for this period is 5.1 percent about 95 percent of the time.

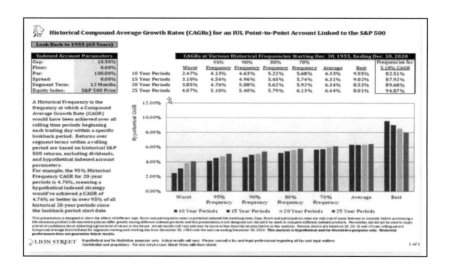

An IUL has a zero percent floor. **Your accumulation value will never lose money.** Market corrections, crashes, and downturns don't cause stress because your principal remains intact. The gains from all the previous years stay locked in, too.

The same is true of another life insurance product, the Fixed Index Annuity. **IULs have caps of 12 to 14** percent. **Most indices have averaged between 5 and 10** percent **over the past twenty-five years. Again, the same is true of a Fixed Index Annuity.**

According to a March 2023 article in LIMRA, "Facing unprecedented long-term market volatility in 2022, consumers sought the protection offered by fixed annuities. Fixed indexed annuity (FIA) sales also had a record quarter and year in 2023. In the fourth quarter, FIA sales were $22.3 billion, a 34% increase from the prior record set in the fourth quarter of 2021. FIA sales were $79.8 billion for the year, up 25% from 2021 and 9% higher than the record set in 2019."

As a part of your retirement journey, UFW believes the safety of your hard-earned assets is vital. The protected lifetime Income of a Fixed Index Annuity can be essential in the high volatility periods we are experiencing now and most likely will continue to do so in the years ahead.

According to an article at protectedincome.org, "Annuities have protected the retirement of millions of Americans over the centuries. Benjamin Franklin saw the power of annuities by giving them to the cities of Philadelphia and Boston in his will. In 2007, then Federal Reserve Chairman Ben Bernanke disclosed that his most significant financial assets were annuities."

HISTORY OF ANNUITIES IN THE U.S.

1930/1940

During the Great Depression, annuities saw a spike in popularity as stock market volatility threatened retirement savings and Americans were looking to protect their assets with more conservative financial products.

1950/1960

During the 1950s, variable annuities rose to prominence, essentially acting as an early version of the contemporary mutual fund. Variable annuities allowed owners to choose their account type and created interest type earnings based on speculative financial vehicles in separate accounts.

1970/1980

Congress passed two important acts in relation to annuities in the early 1980s, the 1982 Periodic Payment Settlement Act and the 1986 Tax Reform Act.

1990/2000

With the turn of the century, a wide variety of products became available. Most notable were the indexed annuity, principal guarantees, and long term care benefits.

PRESENT

Today, with fewer people covered by traditional pension plans, annuities can fill a critical gap in retirement portfolios by providing a guaranteed monthly check for as long as you live, no matter how the markets perform.

There's a reason so many families are making a Fixed Index Annuity a bedrock in their retirement plans.

So, how can you use the advanced strategies of 72(t) to super-charge your IUL Wealth Account, eliminate debt quicker, and build *two* "private pension" funds for your retirement?

Let's dive into this tactic, which can be a part of our Money Max Pro Debt-to-Wealth Strategy.

Suppose you are retired or have moved to another job like many Americans; that money saved in your old company's 401(k) can be rolled over to an IRA without paying taxes. Then, that IRA can be moved to a safe money strategy that can partially fund your wealth-building account. You can move your market-risk 401(k) to a tactic utilizing a Fixed Index Annuity (a life insurance product), which will have protected growth from market losses and build a lifetime income you and your spouse cannot outlive. Too good to be true? Let us show you how.

Case Study III: Robert Tuscon

Robert Tuscon is an I.T. worker who started his career with a small development company after college. His skills were in great demand, and he began a promising job four weeks after graduation. Soon after, he was recruited by one of the Silicon Valley tech start-ups, and after six years with them, a recruiter contacted him on behalf of Tech I. He signed a bonus and was offered excellent benefits, including 401(k), stock options, and a six-figure income. The Seattle campus was exactly what Robert had dreamed of when he spent so many hours working and creating since high school. At thirty-one, he was truly living the dream.

Nothing is for free, and Tech I took its toll: long hours, weekends, and heavy pressure to always take it to the next level. He met his partner, Sanya, a programmer at Tech I. Together, they had the income to purchase a condo in the expensive Seattle real estate market. Life was good; work/life balance was more challenging.

At age thirty-six, Robert decided to quit Tech I and work on his ideas for apps and a unique system for booking reservations at the National Parks using sophisticated algorithms. Booking a campsite less than a year in advance was becoming increasingly difficult. It seemed like everyone was camping these days. With this application, one would know when a site became available before it was publicly advertised and ensure they got the reservation.

Over his three jobs, with the generous company match, Robert and his partner, Sanya, had a total of about $500,000 in their various 401(k)s and an over-concentration in Tech I stock. The markets had become highly volatile, and even Tech I, with its stellar gains during COVID-19, showed some alarming signs of volatility.

Sanya took a work-from-home position with Make a Dream Foundation, and Robert provided private IT support. It left them with a lot of free time to develop the app and to balance the lifestyle that the work at Tech I did not allow.

They had some debt.

Type	Name	Balance	Rate	Remaining	Payment
	BoA	$325,000	4.500 %	30.0-years	$1,897
	Subaru	$35,000	4.200 %	5.0-years	$648
	Student Loan	$50,000	6.000 %	10.1-years	$555
	Citi	$2,000	19.600 %	n/a	$53
	Amex	$23,000	23.900 %	n/a	$688
	All Debts	$435,000	5.743 %	30.0-years	$3,840

And their expenses were reasonable. If only they could eliminate the debt service. That would save them $3,800/month. Robert
knew these loans were front-end loans, and the lenders got their
interest (profit) first as you gradually paid the loans. Banks were
hugely profitable using this kind of money management.

Name	Amount	Frequency	*Base Monthly
Monthly Expenses	$4,500	Monthly	$4,500
Income			$9,748
Expenses		-	$4,500
Debt Payments		-	$3,840
Discretionary Income		=	$1,408

After doing some Google searches and talking to a friend from
Tech I, Kyle, they discovered why Kyle always seemed relaxed
about his future. Like Robert, he had retired early from Tech I and
was working on a personal project. He enjoyed photography and
had been traveling worldwide, taking some exceptional images of
glaciers.

After church, Kyle and his wife Molly shared with Robert and
Sanya how the Money Max Pro Debt-to-Wealth System worked
in their life. At their projected second retirement age of fifty-five,
they would have around $107,000 a year in a private pension fund
created by the Money Max Pro Debt-to-Wealth System every year
until age ninety, as well as provide a death benefit if life got in the
way of their plans, and an extended care provision if they were
critically injured or chronically ill. They were young and healthy,

but everyone knew of someone who had not been as fortunate and ended up in a wheelchair or worse, and unable to work.

Kyle explained that UFF had been eliminating debt for seventeen years by creating financial GPS software that guided a family to the fastest way to zero debt, eliminating all their debt, including those endless student loans, in about ten years. At their annual review a year ago, Kyle and Molly's UFF agent showed them a free upgrade to the Money Max Account they had been using. The Money Max Pro Debt-to-Wealth System took this powerful debt elimination program to a new level. As they paid down their debt, with the program guiding them, they would start building wealth simultaneously.

A permanent high-cash-value life insurance policy was the secret sauce. The special provisions of this policy provide access to the cash value. Then, the accumulation value continues to build for purchases or investments as though you had never withdrawn any funds. This feature allows the Money Max Pro Debt-to-Wealth System to pay off their debt simultaneously and build a healthy retirement fund. And, best of all, with no market risk.

Kyle and Robert both groaned as they recalled 2001–2002 and again in 2008–2009 when their parents had stressed over the enormous losses in their retirement funds in the stock markets. Neither one of them wanted to experience that. The work at Tech I had been arduous, and when they visited a financial planner shortly after they left Tech I, she had them complete a Risk Tolerance Survey. They had to identify whether their risk preference was: conservative, moderate, or high. After reading the questionnaire,

Robert thought, "What they're asking is how much am I willing to lose?" The interviews ended when Robert and Sanya replied, "None. We just worked our buns off for this money. No thanks."

There had to be a better way.

Like Robert and Sanya, Kyle and Molly had 401(k)s when they left Tech I and a small one from a previous employer. The Money Max Pro Debt-to-Wealth System utilized those funds to accelerate its debt elimination and build its wealth plan even faster.

Robert and Sanya were more than a little curious and fascinated. They were good at math and lived in spreadsheets. They knew they could pay off their debt faster by making additional payments to their mortgage, but it was complicated to stay the course as "things" in life interrupted. This Financial GPS and Wealth Building System took the stress and endless spreadsheets out of the formula.

Kyle gave them the contact information for their UFF/UFW agent and promised to be available if they had other questions.

They called and set a Zoom meeting date to review the system and see if it might fit them.

Their UFF/UFW agent collected some of their financial information and showed them their analysis. It was even better than they had anticipated.

Your Personalized Savings Report

| For: Robert Tuscon (age 38)
rj@gmail.com | Debt-Free Goal:
Mar 2043 | Prepared By: Jason Ingram
jason@ingramconsulting.com / (352) 871-3162 | Page 1
Sun Aug 6, 2023 |

Summary of Debts

Name	Balance	Rate	Payment
Mortgage Debt (1)	$325,000.00	4.50%	$1,896.73
Loans (2)	$85,000.00	5.26%	$1,202.84
Credit Cards (2)	$25,000.00	23.56%	$740.82
Total	$435,000.00	5.74%	$3,840.39

Discretionary Income Analysis

Description	Amount	% of Income
Base Monthly Income	$9,748.00	100.0%
Monthly Debt Payments	$3,840.39	39.4%
Other Monthly Expenses	$4,500.00	46.2%
Term	$37.86	0.4%
Monthly Discretionary Income	$1,407.61	14.4%

Having debt is no walk in the park!

This month you'll pay over $2,000 in interest alone. That's 58% of your monthly payment ...gone!

On average over the next 34.6 years your bank's plan will cost you more than $800 per month in interest.

You'll spend $3.85 for every $1 you pay down in principal on your mortgage this month.

It will be September 2038 (when you are 53 years old) before you have paid off half of your debt and you will still owe over $216,000.

What The Money Max Account Pro can do for you

Your Bank's Plan	VS	The Money Max Account Pro	=	You Save
Total Debt Payments				
$768,472 That's 77% more than your current outstanding balance of $435,000!	vs	$533,026 This is the total amount you will pay to completely eliminate all of your listed debts.	=	$235,447 That's a BIG TIP for the bank! Let's make it 107 payments of $2,200.
Total Interest Payments				
$333,472 That's 2.9 years worth of your entire income of $9,748/month just to cover the interest!	vs	$98,026 You would need an interest rate of 1.40% to pay this little interest on a new 30-year loan!	=	$235,447 Save 71% in interest or 2.9 years worth of your entire income!
Projected Payoff				
34.6 years With 415 payments to go you'll still be making payments when you are 73 years old!	vs	8.9 years You'll be debt-free by age 47 after only 107 payments	=	25.7 years What could you do with 308 months with NO monthly debt payments?
Wealth Accumulation				
$0 You'll be making debt payments for the next 35 years instead of building wealth.	vs	$1,754,154 With The Money Max Account Pro, we'll use your 25.7 years saved to start building wealth!	=	$1,754,154 This is your savings with a 1% return. Imagine your savings at higher rates!

Why wait? Start saving today!

By getting started today you can save over $235,000 in interest payments over the next 8.9 years.

By saving 25.7 years of debt payments you could build more than $1,754,000 in wealth over that same time period!

Each month you delay getting started will cost you $2,200 on average over the next 8.9 years! Don't wait! Start now!

Debt-Free In	Debt-Free By	Years Saved	Total Savings	Avg. Savings/Mo
8.9 years	Jun-2032	25.7	$235,447	$2,200

The UFF/UFW agent, Kelly, had asked them about old 401(k) accounts or IRAs they had from previous work. Robert's 401(k) from Tech I was valued at about $250,000, depending on what the stock market did that month. The company had "given" them a lot of company stock, and the value had increased dramatically over the years. He had rolled it into an IRA when he left Tech I.

Kelly explained to them how, through a little-used IRS provision, 72(t), money could be withdrawn from their IRA even though they were not fifty-nine and a half years old without the usual 10 percent penalty if they followed the guidelines set up by the law.

What Is Rule 72(t)?

According to articles in *U.S. News & World Report*, Rule 72(t) allows retirement account owners to make penalty-free withdrawals before age fifty-nine-and-a-half years if they take the distributions in a specific way. "Rule 72(t) allows retirement account holders to set up regular withdrawals—defined as substantially equal periodic payments by the Internal Revenue Code—over the course of five years or until they turn fifty-nine and a half years, whichever is longer."

Most exceptions to the early withdrawal penalty require that the money be used for a specific purpose, but funds withdrawn via rule 72(t) do not require a specific reason. Typically, younger people can only access retirement account funds for urgent needs like medical emergencies or college tuition. While there are specific rules that must be followed, 72(t) gives a lot more leeway. Funds can be used for any reason.

Robert asked, "Why and how would this benefit us?"

Kelly shared the notes from a presentation she had prepared when she took their financial information.

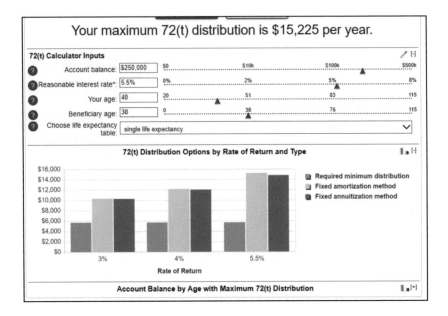

Using this IRS provision, Robert could reposition his IRA into a Fixed Index Annuity (FIA) and begin taking yearly withdrawals of $15,225 a year until he turns sixty. He then "turns on" the lifetime income rider provided by the policy. Using an illustration based upon the last twenty years of the markets, the projected income at age 60 will be $40,026, and each year the index increases, the early income payment will increase. By the time he is 65, the projected income will be $60,650, and at age 75, it will be $141,229 yearly. On an initial $250,000, cumulative withdrawals at age 60 are projected to be $304,500—utilizing Rule 72(t)—before the lifetime income benefit rider will be "turned on." After the yearly lifetime income withdrawals are begun, cumulative withdrawals are projected to be $615,089 at age 65; $1,050,443 at age 70; and $1,566,637 at age 75—all on a $250,000 initial investment!

After all these withdrawals—and even when the account balance is zero—the fixed index annuity will continue to pay the yearly income (with annual increases as the market performs) until the annuitant has passed. What account do you have that will pay you an annual income *after* the balance is zero?

Kelly had an illustration of the FIA and what that would look like using this provision. Courtesy of Athene Insurance Company.

Year Ending	Age	End of Year Age	Partial Withdrawal	Lifetime Income Withdrawals	Cumulative Withdrawals	Benefit Base	Accumulated Value	Death Benefit
1	40	41	$15,225	$0	$15,225	$312,760	$250,290	$250,290
2	41	42	$15,225	$0	$30,450	$420,603	$298,499	$298,499
3	42	43	$15,225	$0	$45,675	$399,150	$283,274	$283,274
4	43	44	$15,225	$0	$60,900	$409,408	$283,905	$283,905
5	44	45	$15,225	$0	$76,125	$419,447	$284,677	$284,677
6	45	46	$15,225	$0	$91,350	$462,837	$302,363	$302,363
7	46	47	$15,225	$0	$106,575	$465,253	$299,999	$299,999
8	47	48	$15,225	$0	$121,800	$596,286	$362,096	$362,096
9	48	49	$15,225	$0	$137,025	$583,270	$352,899	$352,899
10	49	50	$15,225	$0	$152,250	$559,109	$338,175	$338,175
11	50	51	$15,225	$0	$167,475	$574,947	$343,455	$343,455
12	51	52	$15,225	$0	$182,700	$735,168	$421,084	$421,084
13	52	53	$15,225	$0	$197,925	$708,586	$405,859	$405,859
14	53	54	$15,225	$0	$213,150	$723,700	$411,481	$411,481
15	54	55	$15,225	$0	$228,375	$742,230	$418,910	$418,910
16	55	56	$15,225	$0	$243,600	$823,681	$457,899	$457,899
17	56	57	$15,225	$0	$258,825	$835,146	$462,099	$462,099
18	57	58	$15,225	$0	$274,050	$1,076,100	$581,109	$581,109
19	58	59	$15,225	$0	$289,275	$1,066,777	$575,320	$575,320
20	59	60	$15,225	$0	$304,500	$1,039,647	$560,645	$560,645
21	60	61	$0	$40,026	$344,526	$1,027,346	$551,580	$551,580
22	61	62	$0	$42,407	$386,933	$1,250,069	$660,027	$660,027
23	62	63	$0	$54,971	$441,904	$1,145,956	$605,057	$605,057
24	63	64	$0	$54,971	$496,875	$1,093,752	$576,040	$576,040
25	64	65	$0	$57,564	$554,439	$1,040,027	$546,263	$546,263
26	65	66	$0	$60,650	$615,089	$1,068,976	$557,823	$557,823
27	66	67	$0	$69,668	$684,757	$976,325	$508,583	$508,583
28	67	68	$0	$72,583	$757,340	$1,126,445	$580,729	$580,729
29	68	69	$0	$96,677	$854,017	$953,986	$491,585	$491,585
30	69	70	$0	$98,182	$952,199	$763,947	$393,651	$393,651
31	70	71	$0	$98,244	$1,050,443	$605,385	$311,456	$311,456
32	71	72	$0	$103,581	$1,154,024	$532,937	$272,317	$272,317
33	72	73	$0	$135,692	$1,289,716	$267,382	$136,626	$136,626
34	73	74	$0	$135,692	$1,425,408	$1,904	$972	$972
35	74	75	$0	$141,229	$1,566,637	$0	$0	$0

Robert and Sanya's IRA, currently subject to market risks, would be transferred with no taxation to a Fixed Index Annuity, eliminating that market risk and allowing them to take systematic withdrawals utilizing IRS code 72(t). This strategy would increase their discretionary income, eliminate their debt faster, and allow more significant funding for the IUL. An additional benefit would be moving money from a position of risk into one of no risk (market funds to the IUL), and all the gains on those funds transferred to the IUL would grow tax-exempt and come out tax-free in retirement or be available for loans for any purpose they need. They would have created liquidity and flexibility where there was little in their current strategy.

She explained that only the yearly withdrawals allowed under 72(t), $15,225, would be taxable as ordinary income. With a marginal tax rate of 20 percent, their after-tax withdrawal would be $12,180/year. Kelly shared that that would increase their discretionary income and thus eliminate their debt quicker and fund their Wealth Account (IUL) more powerfully, giving them a more significant income when they stop working, not to mention considerable tax advantages.

An Increasing Income on a decreasing asset is unique in the world of financial planning.

When the debt elimination and income strategy were complete, the projected income from the annuity and the IUL would look like this:

Tucson Full book V6
Uploaded: 1/13/2024   Date Prepared: 1/13/2024   Rate Class: Standard Non-Tobacco

Face Value	Initial Premium	Riders
$1,381,801	$6,231 Monthly	ABR, DBPR, LIBR, OPR, SAR

Term Length	Premium
20-G	$29 Monthly

[Hide Report] [Download] [Delete]

Description		Monthly	Annual	Total For Period
Premium	Year 1-6	$6,084	$73,006	$438,036
Loans	Year 2-6	$5,669	$68,028	$340,140
Premium	Year 7-26	$4,998	$59,976	$1,199,520
Income	Age 65-90	$21,479	$257,746	$6,701,396
Max Accumulation	Age 64	$2,487,880			Death Benefit Age 90: $1,240,533

Cash Value at Payoff Year: $36,183   **Total Benefit: $7,941,929**

Compare to Taxed Income: **$343,661** at a Rate of   25 %   Total Premium - Loans $1,297,416

Cash % Available **Y1** 47.71% | **Y2** 70.44% | **Y3** 78.11% | **10 YR Avg** 79.97%   Net Return: $6,644,513

From the Wealth Building Account, they would have a projected yearly income of $257,746 from age sixty until age ninety-three, all tax-free.

The projected income from the Fixed Index Annuity (FIA-IRA) at age sixty-five would be $60,650 yearly, potentially increasing each year, and from the IUL, $257,746 annual tax-free. Their total projected yearly income from just these two strategies at age 65 would be $318,396. By age seventy, the total projected income for the annuity and the IUL would be $355,990. By age eighty, their combined income from the FIA and the IUL is projected to be approximately $487,829/yearly, of which $257,746 would remain tax-free. And their debt of $435,000 would be eliminated.

Here's their Wealth Report:

Your Personalized Savings Report

For: Robert Tuscon (age 38) rj@gmail.com	Debt-Free Goal: Mar 2043	Prepared By: Jason Ingram jason@ingramconsulting.com / (352) 871-3162	Page 1 Sat Jan 13, 2024

Summary of Debts

Name	Balance	Rate	Payment
Mortgage Debt (1)	$325,000.00	4.50%	$1,896.73
Loans (2)	$85,000.00	5.26%	$1,202.84
Credit Cards (2)	$25,000.00	23.56%	$740.82
Total	$435,000.00	5.74%	$3,840.39

Monthly Discretionary Income Analysis

Description	Amount	% of Income
Base Monthly Income	$9,748.00	100.0%
Monthly Debt Payments	$3,840.39	39.4%
Other Monthly Expenses	$4,500.00	46.2%
Index Universal Life	$1,230.00	12.6%
Term	$29.13	0.3%
Discretionary Income	$148.48	1.5%

Having debt is no walk in the park!

This month you'll pay over $2,000 in interest alone. That's 58% of your monthly payment ...gone!

On average over the next 34.6 years your bank's plan will cost you more than $800 per month in interest.

You'll spend $3.85 for every $1 you pay down in principal on your mortgage this month.

It will be February 2039 (when you are 53 years old) before you have paid off half of your debt and you will still owe over $216,000.

What The Money Max Account Pro can do for you

Your Bank's Plan	VS	The Money Max Account Pro	=	You Save
Total Debt Payments				
$768,472 That's 77% more than your current outstanding balance of $435,000!	vs	$505,025 This is the total amount you will pay to completely eliminate all of your listed debts.	=	$263,447 That's a BIG TIP for the bank! Let's make it 65 payments of $4,053.
Total Interest Payments				
$333,472 That's 2.9 years worth of your entire income of $9,748/month just to cover the interest!	vs	$70,025 You would need an interest rate of 1.02% to pay this little interest on a new 30-year loan!	=	$263,447 Save 79% in interest or 2.3 years worth of your entire income!
Projected Payoff				
34.6 years With 415 payments to go you'll still be making payments when you are 73 years old!	vs	5.4 years You'll be debt-free by age 47 after only 65 payments.	=	29.2 years What could you do with 350 months with NO monthly debt payments?
Wealth Accumulation				
$0 You'll be making debt payments for the next 35 years instead of building wealth.	vs	$2,030,152 With The Money Max Account Pro, we'll use your 29.2 years saved to start building wealth!	=	$2,030,152 This is your savings with a 1% return. Imagine your savings at higher rates!

Why wait? Start saving today!

By getting started today you can save over $263,000 in interest payments over the next 5.4 years.

By saving 29.2 years of debt payments you could build more than $2,030,000 in wealth over that same time period!

Each month you delay getting started will cost you $4,053 on average over the next 5.4 years! Don't wait! Start now!

Debt-Free In	Debt-Free By	Years Saved	Total Savings	Avg. Savings/Mo
5.4 years	May-2029	29.2	$263,447	$4,053

Robert and Saya had one more question, "How do we get started?"

SECTION 5: CONCLUSION

"In the beginner's mind there are many possibilities, in the expert's mind there are few." -Shunryu Suzuki

IN THE INTRODUCTION to this writing, I asked, "When would you want to know if what you thought was true turned out not to be?"

What was your answer to that question? I'm guessing you thought either "now" or "yesterday."

Would it be a ridiculous thought that you could build wealth and simultaneously eliminate debt by using the same dollar for both?

The Money Max Pro Debt-to-Wealth System is genuinely revolutionary, but at the same time, the strategy uses age-old proven tactics to eliminate debt and build wealth simultaneously. It's just math utilizing a one-of-a-kind debt elimination software to act as your guide.

Will it work for you?

If you are a lifetime learner; if you are sick and tired of banks profiting from your hard-earned money; if you are curious; if you hunger to avoid falling into the same old ways the banks have taught us how to borrow and save, then this strategy is for you.

Who is not suitable for this?

If you don't care; if you won't take a short time to learn how money works and how to leverage those concepts; if you are just too busy and think you already know it all or can do it yourself, it's not for you.

But if you're hungry, humble, and intelligent, you will have a UFF/UFW agent run your analysis.

What do you have to lose? Just your debt and a tax-advantaged retirement.

Have the mind of a beginner; you might be surprised.

APPENDIX 1

Understanding Interest Crediting

Indexed Universal Life (IUL) offers death benefit protection and the potential for cash surrender value accumulation based, in part, on interest credited from a market index

In addition to the death benefit, IUL insurance also offers the potential to build cash surrender value, on a tax-deferred basis, which may be accessed income tax-free during your lifetime through policy withdrawals and loans.

The cash surrender value accumulation is dependent on the interest crediting rates paid by the insurance company on the premiums in excess of the insurance costs. In addition to the fixed interest crediting strategy, some IUL products offer the option to have interest credited based on the changes in the S&P 500® Index, US Pacesetter Index, and Credit Suisse Balanced Trend Index.

How do the indexed strategies' cap and participation rates work?

The indexed strategies credit interest by measuring changes in the S&P 500® Index, US Pacesetter Index, or Credit Suisse Balanced

Trend Index. IUL products do not directly invest in the indexes or in any other securities.

Each indexed strategy has a participation rate. The participation rate determines what percentage of the index change is used in the calculation of credited interest. The participation rate can be less than, greater than, or equal to 100%.

Some of the strategies also have a cap rate. The cap rate limits the amount of interest that a strategy will credit.

Index Crediting Strategies

Indexed strategy credited interest is determined by applying the participation and cap rates to the change in the selected index. First, the change in the index is determined. This is measured over the course of a year. If the change is positive, your policy is credited interest after applying any caps and participation rates. If the change is negative, your policy is credited 0% unless you elect the 1% Floor Strategy, in which case your policy would receive a 1% credit.

Any credited interest is added to your chosen interest-crediting strategies based on the accumulated value at the end of the year. This means you have the potential to earn compound interest, further growing your cash value. Monthly policy expenses will be deducted from the accumulated value prior to the calculation of interest credits.

Point-to-Point

The starting index value is compared to the ending index value exactly one year later, on the 14th of the 12th month. If the ending value is less than the starting value, the interest credit is the floor, which is either 0% or 1%, depending on the strategy. This is the guaranteed floor of the indexed strategies and is often referred to as the "downside protection" offered by indexed products.

If the ending value of the index is greater than the initial value, the percent change is calculated — (the ending value) / (the beginning value) – 1 = the % change.

Cap-Focused and Participation-Focused Strategies:

If % change times the Participation Rate > Cap, then the interest credited is the cap rate.

If % change times the Participation Rate < Cap, then interest is credited based on the change in the index value and the Participation Rate. If the change is negative, the guaranteed floor of 0% or 1% (depending on the indexed strategy) credited will be exercised.

Which strategy is best?

Many people assume that the strategy with the highest illustrated rate will perform the best because maximum illustrated rates are determined by historical index results. However, past performance is not an indicator of future performance.

There is no way to know which indexed strategy will perform the best, either over the long term or the short term.

In addition to indexed strategies, the fixed-term strategy is a fixed-interest strategy that credits a declared interest rate. It is not reliant on any index. Any amount of policy value and premium payments can be allocated to the fixed account.

Allocations can also be divided among some or all of the strategies. There is no way to predict which strategy will perform the best, but by spreading the Allocation across all of the strategies, you can potentially capture at least some of the best returns.

When paying a large single premium or lump sum, as in a 1035 exchange, it may be prudent to allocate a portion to the fixed-term strategy. Then, funds could be periodically moved from the fixed-term strategy to the indexed strategies.

A different way to accomplish this is to use the Systematic Allocation Rider, 6, which can be added to any of our indexed universal life policies. Systematic Allocation allows your clients to use a lump sum or 1035 exchange and spread the strategy allocations over a 12-month period rather than dumping them into the strategies all at once.

Interest Bonus

The Interest Bonus begins in policy year 6. The enhancement is guaranteed to be 0 .35% but may be higher and may vary by crediting strategy.

The Interest Bonus is credited on the policy anniversary. The total Interest Bonus is based on the average accumulated value in each strategy over the prior year. The interest bonus is extra interest calculated on this average value. The extra interest is placed in the Basic Strategy when credited. The Standard Loan Collateral Account does not receive the Interest Bonus.

How do the companies invest to provide indexed credits?

Insurance companies do not invest directly in the S&P 500®, the Credit Suisse Balanced Trend Index, or the US Pacesetter Index to provide indexed strategy credited rates. They transact in options to provide indexed credits as part of an investment strategy known as hedging. Hedging is an investment technique designed to reduce or eliminate financial risk.

To deliver indexed credits, we purchase one-year calls on the indices in sufficient quantity to cover the portion of account value eligible to receive indexed credits. If the index increases, we exercise our call options and receive amounts needed to cover our indexed credited obligations.

On strategies with cap rates, it is possible to offset the cost of purchasing the necessary call options by simultaneously selling call options. The calls we sell give the excess return of the index, above what is needed to cover our interest crediting expenses, to the purchaser of the call. The company does not profit from our hedging strategy. They only use hedging to provide indexed-linked interest crediting.

How are the cap and participation rates determined?

Cap and participation rates are determined by several factors. The most obvious factor is the price of options. Generally, as option prices increase, Cap and participation rates decrease. A number of financial factors cause option prices to increase. An important driver of option costs is index volatility. The more volatile the underlying index is, the higher the option costs are. The index price level, the risk-free interest rate, and the option "strike" price are also factors in determining option prices.

Because Indexed Universal Life is a fixed insurance product, it is backed by assets in our General Account. These assets earn investment income. However, the amount of this investment income can vary as interest rates change. Generally, the more investment income the company earns, the more we have to purchase options, and the higher our cap and participation rates will be. In times of depressed investment earnings, the less they have to spend on options to back the indexed strategies, the lower our cap and participation rates will be.

How are renewal cap and participation rates determined?

For products with one-year strategy terms, our renewal cap and participation rates have been the same as our new money rates. The determination of the renewal rates for one-year strategies is identical to the determination of the rates for new money.
All of the indexed products are managed on a portfolio rate basis. This means that all assets backing the cash value and all investment income from those assets are aggregated.

How are maximum illustrated rates determined?

The maximum illustrated rates for each strategy are determined by applying an industry regulation. This involves applying our current

Cap and participation rates to every hypothetical 25-year index return sequence for the past 65 years to determine an average return.

They model the returns as though our products had been available for the past 65 years and assume that money was deposited each month for each 25-year "look-back" period. The average annual return is calculated and adjusted and becomes the maximum illustrated rate. "Back-casting" to determine maximum illustrated rates only estimates the strategies' hypothetical historical results and can't be used to predict future results. In addition, some states limit the maximum rate allowed to be illustrated on indexed products, so illustrations in those states will reflect that limit.

How often can you make changes to strategy allocations?

Allocations can be changed at any time. But money already in a strategy will only be reallocated according to any changes at the end of the strategy term.

What is the Basic Strategy?

The Basic Strategy is a fixed interest crediting account where any unallocated premium is held until it is moved into your chosen index crediting strategies on the 14th of every month.

How do loans work?

Policy loans are a contractual right. Once the policy has been in force for one year, the policy owner has the right to borrow money from the insurance company by using the policy cash surrender value as collateral for the loans (1035 money is available in year 1). Other than having sufficient policy cash surrender value to use as collateral, there is no condition on being able to borrow money from the insurance company.

Because the insurance company is lending and needs to earn a return on its assets, loan interest is charged on the amount borrowed. This interest can be paid as it is due, or it can be "capitalized" by adding it to the amount borrowed, thus increasing the policy loan.

The Participating Variable and Standard Loans use variable loan interest rates. Variable loan rates may not exceed an amount determined from the current Moody's Composite Yield on seasoned corporate bonds. Current variable loan rates are determined monthly by the company. However, for a given policy, the loan rate is only reset annually on the policy anniversary.

Participating Loan provisions mean that loan collateral remains in indexed strategies and earns indexed interest credits even while being used as loan security. The loan interest rate is charged normally. So, in times when indexed interest credits exceed policy loan interest rates, IUL policy owners will actually earn more on collateral amounts than they are charged on the loan amounts. The opposite condition, or being "upside down," can be very harmful to the insurance policy. Loans should be managed carefully.

An owner can switch the loan type once per policy year without paying off the existing loan. This can be a policy-saving difference if loans ever go upside down.

There are a couple of things to remember about policy loans:

1 . Insurance deductions continue even if there is a loan, so sufficient unloaned cash surrender account value must remain, or extra premium payments may need to be made to continue coverage; otherwise, a policy may lapse, causing adverse tax consequences on loan amounts already received and loss of the policy and coverage.

2 . Policy loan amounts reduce cash surrender values and policy death benefits.

3 . Loans can be repaid. Amounts meant for loan repayment should be clearly designated as such; otherwise, they will be considered premium payments.

How do withdrawals work?

In contrast to a policy loan, withdrawals are an actual removal of cash surrender value from the policy. Withdrawals may be taken for any amount up to the cash surrender value of the policy, less 3 monthly deductions. There is currently no withdrawal fee assessed on withdrawals. However, we may charge as much as $25 per year.

The portion of the cash surrender value that consists of premiums paid into the policy is known as "basis," with any amounts above that considered gains. Cumulative withdrawals up to the basis amount are non-taxable, provided premiums were paid with after-tax money. Withdrawal amounts above basis are taxable as income. Once the basis is withdrawn from a policy, it is usually advisable to switch to loans to access any additional cash surrender value. This avoids any immediate tax consequence, but it is important to keep the policy in force; otherwise, the loans become taxable on policy lapse.

Account Strategies

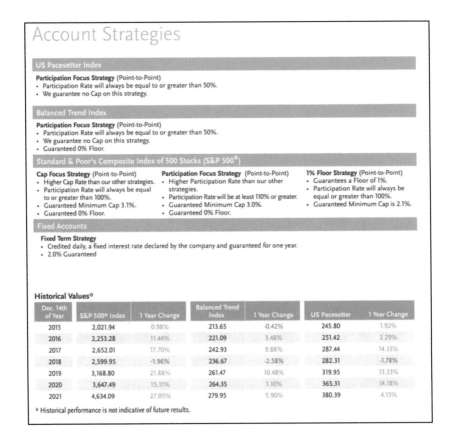

DISCLOSURE

Information current as of October 30, 2023.

Opinions, estimates, forecasts, and statements of financial market trends that are based on current market conditions constitute our judgment and are subject to change without notice.

This material is for information and educational purposes only and is not intended as an offer or solicitation with respect to the purchase or sale of any security.

Consult your financial professional before making any investment decisions.

All information is believed to be from reliable sources; however, we make no representation as to its completeness or accuracy.

Made in United States
Troutdale, OR
06/21/2025

32273608R00051